All
Those Mothers
at the
Manger

Norma Farber
illustrated by
Megan Lloyd

All Those Mothers at the Manger

Harper & Row, Publishers

All Those Mothers at the Manger
Text copyright © 1979 by Norma Farber
Illustrations copyright © 1985 by Megan Lloyd
This poem originally appeared in *Cricket* magazine.
Printed in the U.S.A. All rights reserved.
Designed by Al Cetta
1 2 3 4 5 6 7 8 9 10
First Edition

Library of Congress Cataloging in Publication Data
Farber, Norma.
  All those mothers at the manger.

  "Originally appeared in Cricket magazine"—T.p. verso.
  Summary: Animal mothers gathered around a young woman
giving birth to her child in a stable let her know that no mother
is a stranger to another anywhere.
  1. Children's stories, American. [1. Jesus Christ—
Nativity—Fiction. 2. Christmas—Fiction. 3. Mothers—
Fiction. 4. Domestic animals—Fiction. 5. Stories in
rhyme] I. Lloyd, Megan, ill. II. Title.
PZ8.3.F224Al 1985   [E]   85-42610
ISBN 0-06-021869-X
ISBN 0-06-021870-3 (lib. bdg.)

All those mothers at the manger—
hen and cow and mare and ewe—

gathered round the lovely stranger
while her baby still was new.

All those mothers at the manger—
cow and mare and ewe and hen—

934

welcomed warm the lovely mother,
welcomed soft her baby then.

All those mothers at the manger—
mare and ewe and hen and cow—

praised the lovely little stranger:

perfect features, peaceful brow.

All those mothers at the manger—

ewe and hen and cow and mare—

said, *No mother is a stranger*
to another

anywhere.